Love Is a Stone Endlessly In Flight

To pat,
fellow fan of Irish poetry

yours in friendship

Dante Di Stefano

Love Is a Stone Endlessly In Flight

Poems

by

Dante Di Stefano

BRIGHT
HORSE
BOOKS

Brighthorse Books
13202 North River Drive
Omaha, NE 68112

ISBN: 978-1-944467-02-9

Cover Design: Christina Di Stefano

For Christina

In memoriam
Dominic Di Stefano Jr.
and
David Bosnick

Love that is a stone endlessly in flight
so long as stone shall last bearing
the chisel's stroke...

—William Carlos Williams
(*Paterson*, Book Two, Section I)

Contents

Statue of the Emaciated Buddha

The cloth that drapes his loins is like a bow
a hunter might draw back against a buck
in a Pennsylvania boondock woods.
His veins trace turnpikes over jutting bones
and lids remain closed as if the cosmos
had become an obsidian speck wormed
beneath the almond blossoms of his eyes.
From the center of this black stony mass
the whole world plummets like a meteor
of curses and wishes the wind casts off
in the moments before enlightenment.
A billion starlings go spinning out
into the night. Doves don't murmur inside
the temple. Bullshit. Forget your life. Fast.

Channeling Mingus

Sometimes I rage at the laziness America
stamps on the melody of alleys and moonlight.
Then, I get to talking from the bandstand
and I realize I can't recall the secrets the crickets
in Watts once rolled out sideways for me.

I glorify bus rides and speak in shotgun shells
to the bullshit a shooting star spits across
the sky and I remember that the whale's
ribcage is the true baseline of the Nineveh
I seek in my instrument's anarchic ramblings.

Oh yeah, I'll just play on despite the angels
and their incessant racket. I'll call the hogs
and feed them the slop of the sky blue darkness
that's chugging through my gut and wringing
my desire out to dry on the clothesline

of a riff that's gonna flummox God and send
His cracker ass spinning through eternity,
where he can talk to the devil about how
I'm not one black cat, but three, skulking
verve to the blandishments of the cosmopolitan.

If I was a Character in a Rural Noir I'd Learn Claw Hammer Banjo and Mourn the Slow Betrayal of the Body that Inevitably Occurs in Life Outside of Novels

after Tom Bouman

When the wind shakes the bottle tree's branches
and sets the empty old pints to clinking,
a bleak in my lack breaks into a want
I can't staunch and can't scarcely understand.

The shack I call a home reeks of bat piss
and creosote. There's murder in the elms.
The lye-caked cracks in my palms recall pains
and a picket fence rots by the roadside.

God, if he's listening, presses his ear
to the bole sprout that sprung from a black knot
of the last maple before the power line cut
on the hill beside the collapsed pole barn.

At nighttime, the bullfrogs deliver us
a sermon, more deliberate than song,
and there's nobody to hear it except
my regrets, my thirty ought six, and me.

Of course, I still believe in the glory
of birches and the memory of love
is like a leaf that doesn't skitter off
the burn barrel's kerosene doused trash.

In the tree-stand I sit dabbed with the scent
of doe and waiting for the stag in me

to hurdle the underbrush, but he comes
no closer than the edge of this boscage.

When you see a fire blaze on the east ridge,
realize it might consume you; know chance
keeps you alive, cricket music is poor,
saplings don't have to grow, and roots may die.

Notice how blue spruce marshals golden light:
to endure you've got to be as stubborn
and as crazy as a shithouse rat;
break fiddles if you must, get drunk, and dance.

Love is a Stone Endlessly in Flight

The Great Falls strike their silk upon bullheads
and trout my father never fished for there;
he was about other rivers and falls,
about other waters' vagrant currents
calling him home, calling him Dominic,
telling stories of a man forever
a boy in photographs from the fifties,
wearing a cowboy hat with a cap gun
cocked in his hand. The Passaic River
didn't call him, but the Chenango did;
it cut like a glacier through the basalt
of millennia. Oh Paterson, Oh
Williams, what I mean to say is just this:
my father's people made their way through trades,
as dishwashers and factory workers,
in a city that had no Passaic
to buttress it; they, and he, were always
skipping stones in elsewhere rushing eddies,
dreaming flocks they wouldn't tend and orchards
full of apples they could never harvest.
Oh rivers of the world, my father died
in my arms as I carried him, almost
to the hospice bed. It was an honor
to stoop and cradle him on the threshold
of the afterlife, where he, I hope, skips
stones with the broken vowels of immigrant
angels. Holy green waters that roll on
forever, when I went to his fresh grave
I wanted to lay down on the flowers
and sleep there, or hug the dirt, but instead
I sifted through the packed soil and found

four flat pebbles to give to my mother
because the stone lives, the flesh dies, and we
know nothing of death or its mills that churn
into a place that is not home. Great Falls,
strike your silk upon the bullheads and guide
my father to a street lined with linden
where the difficult labor of living
is done. Oh spent shell from the final
volley, I hold you in my palm and I know
no metaphor can honor a father.
"A chance word," Williams said, "upon paper,
may destroy the world." Dear dad, I write you
exact words dictated by the whirlpool
that forms at the confluence of other rivers:
Yes, love is a stone endlessly in flight.

The Orchard Keeper

My father wanted to be an apple orchard.
To this end he spent thirty years tortured
by the hum of letter sorting machines,
which shuffled neither rain, nor sleet, nor snow,
nor hail, until his face assumed the sheen
of a red delicious, whose sorrow
the worm only knows.

A Defense of Confessional Poetry

You might fabricate a fallen empire
by the sway of tall grass in an orchard.
By you I mean I and I mean to tell you
that clocks in hospitals look like Chagall's
at three-thirty in the morning Tuesdays
when your father snores in the bed unaware
of the cancer that has blocked his bile ducts
and jaundiced even the whites of his eyes.
It is then that the minute hand fishlike
dips below the current of a greater
grief, which causes the man in the next bed
to call for both his mother and daughter
just before he wets himself and shrieks "Oh God,
why me?" Of course, like the phrase "like clockwork,"
God turns dead metaphor and coasts the current
of a greater grief, which I can only say
by noting the dried blood splotched on the gown
I have re-tied for my father five times
by five-thirty on this Tuesday morning.
You might sway the tall grass in an orchard
by staring at the fake stained glass decal
they stuck to a window that looks out on
a brick wall, in order to hide the fact
that each patient's another Bartleby,
meaning another empty marker stamped
with an "I would prefer not to" that navigates
the current of a greater grief, or God.
However, this is just an unclear way
for a son, whom both you and I well know
cannot yet speak his sorrows to the stones
at orchard edge, to tell of how he felt

when his father told him that he wanted
to die and that he dreamt heaven a roof
at the post office where he worked for years,
thirty years, and on this roof his mother
danced with her arms open, calling him home
to dance in the open air, in a place
without clocks or hospitals, where hearses
don't stop, and his face has not wasted a shade
of yellow, the color of which has only
been known in the tints of Chagall's tall grasses
and in the lost fabrics woven during
the declining years of a fallen empire.

Making a Canoe Out of the Eden Tree

It rained the first time I saw my mother cry.
Her cheek was pressed against a blue couch,
the tears splotched between paisley patterns
like a patch of Queen Anne's Lace in ragweed.
Meanwhile, my father painted the kitchen
the color of a postal shirt, stood on his head
in a yoga pose, and dangled Benson & Hedges
menthol 100s in his hand of god of Sicily.

Marionettes hung from all corners and leered
in the glow of nightlights. In fact, everything
was yellow and looming, but I was unafraid.

Sunlight tiptoed past the stained glass window
on the landing of the stairs, tagged me lightly,
and said, "you're it." Try as I might, I couldn't
catch him. Instead, I climbed the high steps
and ate an apple in the attic. How lustrous
it was, even in the halo of a 40 watt bulb.

With a Coat

I was cold and leaned against the big oak tree
as if it were my mother wearing a rough apron
of bark, her upraised arms warning of danger.
Through those boughs and leaves I saw
dark patches of sky. I thought a brooding
witch waited to catch me up from under
branches and take me, careening on her broom,
to her home in the jaundiced moon.
I looked to the roof of mom and dad's house
and wondered if the paisley couch patterns
would change during the day. My brother peeked
from a window and waved. When the bus came,
I pawed away from the trunk, fumbled,
and took my first step toward not returning.

Seventeen

At night I lie out on the garage roof
and look at pine trees, the same old new stars
perched on the pitch of the sky. Creek's voice
covered by train noise covers my father's house
with calm. In the kitchen, a light comes on
and fills the small frame of the window.
My father walks to the fridge in boxers
and undershirt. His mind's all orchard rot,
and linnet wings flaring in a darkling glare.
I shrink closer to the slant of the roof,
blue skin on my eyelids, wings hid, ready
to drink fireflies from a dropper, moonlight
mixed with milk of stars and crickets,
fed by flight of 2 A.M. turning.

Accident Report

Frogs swim in my forearms as I try to unbuckle the seatbelt.
My neck is an empty church pew. My eyelids are sacks of
crushed glass. Shadows of tree branches cross in the blinking
of a taillight.

Once, my father picked a purple flower. "They sprout unex-
pectedly in any season," he said. He gave it to my mother.

I exit through the smashed upside down passenger door,
through crumpled airbags and smoke. Salamanders crawl
through my calves and scurry into my thighs as I walk away
from the wreck.

"The angels are always with you," my mother once said.

As I walk away, I touch a piece of windshield in my pocket,
a relic, a fish in the communion cup. No one stops as I try
to hitch a ride. My arms and legs are estuaries. My torso, a
hewn tree.

Tonight, I will sleep outside. The face of God is just this: the
difficulty of turning the wheel while the angel wrenches your
hip from the socket.

Chemotherapy Epithalamion

He said he heard an owl as he drifted
from nightlight, past midnight moon,
to hospital hallway and back again.
The infant wisps of his silver hair called
for the comb of a hand to stroke strands
back in place. He mumbled to the dark
the refrain, "To go far is to return."
He hugged the honeycomb of the pillow
and said "Gina, let's go to the beach."
But when he woke and looked around the room
the comb of her hand had gone for good.
"What is this shit?" he said and smiled (and smiled).
Meanwhile, the wing of a thing mistaken
for a bride began to beat, rise, and glide.

From Nightlight Past Midnight Moon to Hospital Hallway and Back Again

Her grave's remained unmarked for a month now.
They're waiting for May, for the ground to thaw,
for the birds to come, for the weather to shift
so the tombstone won't. My dad took a picture
of the plot and said, "She looks nice, doesn't she?"
He showed me the picture in its paper frame.
My answer came yearning verdant through the dead
grass, wishing to green the wind inside the wind.
He said, "I can carry her with me anywhere now."
He handed it to me. I held it to the sky. He said,
"It's real nice for her here." I said I thought so too.
He put a wreath on the spot where she lies. The wind
keeps blowing it away and he keeps chasing after it
and finding it and putting it back in place.

Field Trip

On a day my father almost died,
I watched middle school children parade
by the window of the cab I sat in
as we waited for the light to turn
and York Avenue opened up like his sutures,
poorly stitched. I watched them walk on tiptoes,
woodwinds under their arms, necks free
of lacerations, tracheae intact.
I saw them disappear down 68th Street
and thought of the orchids that surround
all the waiting rooms in Sloan-Kettering,
how their heads dip downward, as if heaven
were a hollow beneath the earth.

Filibuster to Delay the Death of My Father

And so my view—and I think it reflects
the view of the American people—
is that we, of course, want to legislate
the nipples of dew that linger on the tips
of grass, but since we've culled the rhetoric
of longing from our tongue, we have seen fit
to let the Fed loan funds to gravity.
No longer can we depend on autumn
to drift in through the window as cinder
and what we need now is to rip parting
from the lexicon, to borrow against
the falsetto hymns the seraphim sing.
I want to be another Abraham,
glutted by stars and wayward with desire.
My two uncles talk the republican
ticket on those remembered front porches
where my dad smoked menthol cigarettes,
always a bit removed, grazing twilight
with his eyes and dreaming orchards, Edens
chased after, that slivered into comets.
The squirrels in my backyard squabble over
crabapples and the strength of a father
echoes the terrible might of the dying.
If only I could unseal covenants.
If only I could chrism concrete, summon
ghosts, conjure living rooms, conjugate time
with the body of a brown haired woman
whose areolas unloose history.
When my father read me the *Aeneid*,
I knew one day I would out walk the sacked
and burning place he came from, forever

carrying his weight until he became
the very trudge made toward not founding
a glorious city in an empire
of ash. Stooping: this is how a father
builds a son. Then a son staggers father,
stutters his father into multitudes.
Once, in a diner, he said he saw life
as a perpetual locking out. "Look
in the windows," he said, "and break them, pane
after pane." And so, in my view, we want,
of course, communion and the promise
of pacts fulfilled, but no nation, no god,
no treaty, can unbind what shuttles son
to live and live and shoulder this breaking.

Channeling Nina Simone

Because America is all about the backlash
and I am comping toward the future,
I don't expect you to commiserate
with me worth a Mississippi goddam.
I carry on contralto and deny
the depthless vertigo of gratitude.
I wish I knew how it feels to be free,
but the king of love is dead and gone now.
Don't want to know prayer, don't want to know man,
beast, burden, woman slung with child, or what's burst
into the southern drawl a state trooper
spits onto the pavement of a highway.
I sing for parents forced to the back row
of the recital hall. I am throated
with places my voice would raze to shining:
Asheville, Harlem, Monrovia, Paris.
There was no reason and there was no cause
for the haunted logic of the bullwhip
to hobble out the national anthem
little girls and little boys drone in school.
I will not hum their buckshot, tie nooses
with their lyrics, or mouth their crooning doused
with gasoline. Instead, I turn my tongue
into a cudgel and chant against what
batters the great truths buried in a tune.
Melody's my hammer; my holy ghost
building, a sliver of dawn turned to psalm,
caroled like the report of a pistol,
echoing in the ears of a bloodhound.
I'm through with cotton dresses, through waiting
for the night to whine my requiem.

When a lovely ache punches my gut,
and I bear the gap no harmonies cross,
up I jump, a face afire like sunset,
belting countries lit with insurgent notes.

Fighting Weather

In May, the bluebirds scuffle from branches
and a lone black crow on the tall oak eats
a carrion sparrow whole like a host
an elderly communicant swallows.
There's a lawn to mow out front and a popped
tire to mend on the bicycle hanging
from the wall in the garage. The sun beats
time on asphalt. The breeze provokes the blades
of grass that have grown too high near the curb.
The grass has grown over my father's grave
and all of my old complaints against him
have gone underground the way that the rain
dissipates into the water table.
I will not argue with his coughing ghost.
I am a small boy no older than five.
My father drives as if fleeing from God,
or some unknown tributary of rage,
flowing with the winding dirt roads we ride.
The scenery quarrels in the rearview.
There, the afterlife of a snow angel drifts
in a spot on the slope of yard where arms
broke fresh powder into wings and legs burst
flakes into a dress's crinoline bell,
but no hint of halo stays to tell me
what heaven has written upon the thaw.
Now, I genuflect to sunlight coming
through the far door and I mourn my father.
There is an electric bill to pay yet
on the coffee table, hedges to clip,
and the sound of somebody jumping rope
comes in through the window like braided smoke.

I'd like for once to tear down the twitter
of a scarlet tanager in midflight,
to make that burry repetitive trill
my own, to render my chest a barrel
over falls the rocks break to smithereens.

Without Wings

after Milton Kessler

When my dad began dying and no pebble,
no ocean, no altar, could hold my grief,
I went through his dresser drawers
to find my legacy in pill bottles filled
with buffalo nickels and wheat pennies,
shoe boxes stuffed with bills and postal badges,
Cialis in plastic packets, holy cards
from funeral masses, his mother's rings
neatly folded in his father's handkerchief,
grey notebooks with the hieroglyphic
script of his Palmer Method cursive,
which related dreams of apple orchards
and untried schemes to get rich quick,
love letters he'd sent to my mother,
signed Giovanni, which was not his name,
nubs of pencils bound in rubber bands,
neckties with price tags still attached
and boxer shorts still in their packaging,
photographs documenting 1942,
Linden Street, the old Italians whose names
no longer ring out like communion bells,
an address book scribbled with residences
that no longer belong to family and friends,
dog tags from World War II and Vietnam
at rest in the reliquary of a Melachrino cigarette tin
along with two Ballantine beer bottle openers,
pleated pants stained with tea tree oil,
work shirts that smelled of attic and smoke,
tattered socks twisted around each other
like the Caduceus or a double helix,

and my DNA's accumulated weight arranged
in bundles and bric-a-brac that will never
be sorted out, catalogued, or bequeathed.
I have never known him well enough, never will,
and yet I see him juking through the defense
on the ten yard line at the old north high stadium,
his legs pounding like hammers against iron girders,
no angel, no wind, no memory holding him back,
and I, a small stone, stuck in his cleat,
knocked loose on the goal line and unaware
of how I'd been picked up and carried so far.

Stephen Hawking Warns Artificial Intelligence Could End Mankind

There is no algorithm to explain
away suffering or to reanimate
the skitter a leaf makes as it crosses
a boyhood memory of idleness,
rustling the dark vestibules of autumn,
and the most disturbing part of the brain
turned positronic is that indolence
would dwindle or be rewritten with code,
but what would be lost would skitter there still
in the ether as binary sequence,
the idea that laziness cradles
love and love overrides neural networks
in the same way that one note from Coltrane's
horn could surely undo the universe.

Channeling Coltrane

When the wind jaws you into another
way of seeing, after the icicles
on the low eaves of your garage have cracked
and fallen on the first snow, you beam on
and softly as in a morning sunrise
you reckon this dead fathoming a chord
jabbed into your bloodstream and spooling there.
In other words, there's no wrong note, only
the spires of churches to sermonize doubt
and reel a melody back to before
before, and before that a bluebell beat
to quivering, pursed lips straining to bloom.
Things get complicated theorizing
ascensions, renewals, avowals, truths.
You find yourself falling from the daily.
The arco of everyday talk aches you.
Even the sparrow's birdsong seems played out.
You want what's weightier than the ballads
the breeze gabbles and lodges in your brain
like an old revolver thrust in a desk drawer.
The Holy Spirit no longer careens
through your dusks, but the ghost of a blessing
stirs in your platelets when you pedigree
a rhythm daybreaking into *amen*.
Charlie Parker put country music on
the jukebox because he loved those stories
that sprung like rust from fender and then spun
from vinyl groove to needle to speaker
to eardrum, breaking him back to the place
he'd come from and couldn't call home; of course,
that's the dilemma all musicians face:

the first failure of homecoming starts when
you utter *home* at the end of a phrase.

Dancing in the Parking Lot of the *Prefabricati*

Chamomile carries you
      down supermarket aisles
           and up cemetery rows

           that rise until you come
      to yourself
swaying, and smiling,

in some gift shop,
      to Willie Nelson,
           and maybe then you're back

           among the little yellow
      one room houses
in your hometown, dancing

to Michael Jackson
      in the moonlight,
           for a moment, when death

           was only a black felt pin
      tacked on a T-shirt.

Benny

When your mother grew ill
you say he knew and kept watch,
curled at her sick bed. He whined,
you say, and licked her toes
like Jesus washing the apostles' feet.

When she died, you tell me
he whimpered in the room
where she took her last breath
and barked from the corner.

In pictures, he looks like a shaggy
little Charlie Chaplin, a mutt
grown mute and wobbly,
a thin old boy who has known
too much pain and fear to keep
his saucer eyes from shivering
into the handwriting of tears.
You long for an irretrievable cursive.

You believe animals have souls
because of this dog and maybe
they do, if souls are the spaces
that fill want with more want
and break a feeling of loss
into one long low throaty howl
in a house I would fill for you
if I could, but which remains
empty except for the angel
figurines that collect dust
in the basement and the angels

who bare their teeth at the sea
less than a mile from its doorstep.

If I Did Not Understand the Glory and Suffering of the Human Heart I Would Not Speak Before Its Holiness

after Saint Theresa of Avila

When I close my eyes I see my father,
dying. I dab his head with a washcloth.
His open mouth jaws a gurgled amen.
His eyes emote hosannas of breakage.

I wish my eyes could blink a drone strike back
into tactical non-being; the dead
ghost down the road in a wedding convoy,
and I wonder how I might turn away
from a deep sorrow that is not my own.
When I fall asleep I don't dream stairwells.
In me, a school of salmon swims upstream.
In me, a fish leaps against the headboard.

Dear Lord, I fear paradise diffuses,
in a sharp gust, like dandelion puff.
Set the tinder of old phrases burning.
I'm waiting to pull the bee from the rose.

I call the door ajar in me a grace.
I want to be as flagrant as the wind
that cuts December Wednesdays in half.
I hear notes that build a more merciful
God, some days, and other days I just let
the bear in my belly swing from my hips
and I paw out my animal blessings.
And my animal blessings paw out me.

Your Freckles Compared to a Muddy Waters Song

after Bei Dao

Between me and the world: you are the one
bent note that breaks a chord into that lack,
the longing of porch swings and honey bees,
which is to say, you sail on, long distance,
through the air with sepals as receivers.

Yeah, those sunlight dabs the good Lord flecked on
your nose, dappled on your chest, and drizzled
on your shoulders make me want to holler
hallelujah, talk about black cat bones,
and grab my Saint John the Conqueror root,

which is to say: between me and the world,
you are a nation that twangs in my gut;
you are what rocking chair does to floor board
when a plucked string sets a body to shining.

While Listening to Professor Longhair I Imagine the Atoms in the Flowers of a Winter Cherry Outside my Windowsill and I Know Everything's Gonna Be Alright

They're whistling "Big Chief" to nucleotides,
lyricizing the fact that love's isotope
decays, as if we didn't know that touch
remains as uncertain as the patterns
of particles larger than hydrogen.
The neutrons are in bloom and the crawdad
fiesta down by the riverside ought
to bring back days of a childhood illness
when the whole world seemed like the breeze a screen
door lets in through the kitchen; time stalls out
and even the cooking utensils take
to flying while your mother and father,
in the other rooms, are forever there,
frozen in their respective youths, but now,
looking back without the basic units
of matter that made a marriage of sperm
and egg, you lose yourself in your language
until music jars you into the grace
of its creolized quantum mechanics
and the patois of the stars and the moon
gets translated into the swing of hips.
Now, the woman you love is like a cloud
of electrons, swirling a new cosmos,
whiplashed by feral tails of galaxies.
The negatively charged cloud wheels around
the nucleus with a barrelhouse strut
fused to a cakewalk that reminds you
every still life is in flight. The sketches

that constitute a poem are rendered
best as invasive species, whose wide root
systems send up tendrils at some distance
from where they were first planted and escape,
in so doing, cultivation. Oh yeah,
protons yell and this wilding process makes
space for faith in a cluster of skin cells
on the tip of a pin. The Japanese
offer the winter cherry's seeds to guide
the souls of the dead. My poor words offer
a papery covering to protect
the decorous waltz of loss that dances
in the molecules of my fingertips.

Let the Mermaids Flirt with Me

When my earthly trials are over, carry my body out in the sea.
Save all the undertaker bills, let the mermaids flirt with me.
——Mississippi John Hurt

In idle moments I expect a chord
might break me into an understanding
with God and music steals nothing from death
when it's played with the finned alacrity
of dangerous swims through such unknowing,
but most days I'm just serving sentences
that unwind like a dictionary of
words spoken by the anemone wind.

Today, I'm mourning my dead whose bodies
sparrow in their caskets under the ground
and the universe seems a motherless
child, quilting a blanket from orphaned light.

Rather than tell my sorrows to the stones,
let this frigate earth wheel and seduce me.

A Carpetbagger's Guide to
Holly Springs, Mississippi

I'd like to say that when I visited the great
Bluesman's grave I said a prayer, drank
a swig of moonshine in tribute, shouted
out the lyrics to "You're Gonna Find
your Mistake," and climbed the line of trees
near the Kimbrough Baptist Church.

I'd like to say that as I stood at the foot
of the grave of the man whose tombstone
reads "Meet me in the City" and "Junior
Kimbrough is the beginning and end
of all music," I could hear his wailing
well up from the Mississippi dust.

I'd like to say it was midnight and moonlight
wrapped me like kudzu while Junior's
voice echoed the imperfect symmetry
of constellations and his guitar wavered
in whispered bursts like autumn breeze
through drooping magnolia leaves.

I'd like to say that I told Junior then that when
I first heard his songs they terrified and undid me
in the best kind of way, cured me like a sick
patient or a Virginia ham, caused me to see
myself the way a stranger does in moments,
and reacquainted me with own brittle bones.

Instead, I'll say that I repeated the same mistakes
I made at William Faulkner's grave and became
the worst kind of tourist, asking my friends

to take a picture of me beside the tiny plot,
posing like a preteen next to the newest
pop sensation postered on her bedroom walls.

Junior, I'm thinking of the loose change
and the broken flower pot left on your grave,
the small wire fence and the patch of dirt
that marks where your body rests, and all
the bric-a-brac of moments that make a life
a Dollar General we shuffle through;

Junior, I'm saving my nickels and dimes,
scanning the shelves, knowing I've got to be
better than the impulse buys of self unfolding
in time or the sad days and lonely nights
of strip malls that define the highways now,
knowing that music begins and ends during

a desire to be better or other than mere catfish
caught in the egret beak of space and time.

What I Learned from Spaghetti Westerns

That the Valle del Treja near Rome can double
for the gray wall canyons of California
and that the Tabernas desert in Spain
can become the Mojave when the camera rolls,

that wasteland and prairie look the same the world over,
that scrub brush and tumbleweed can conjure a myth,
that Italian and Spanish actors may pass as Mexicans
with bandoliers slung over their shoulders,

that confrontations usually end in death,
that death knocks you off the donkey you're riding
and puts a hole in your chest when you least expect it,
that in lieu of a six shooter an axe handle will do,

that serapes and cigarillos and whiskey are hallmarks
of true heroism, but that heroes ride into town
and leave without ever telling anyone their name,
that America has always been a vast mesa

full of outlaws, drunken banditos, and bad acting,
that wherever you go there's a movie score
whistling through your head, that spurs jingle,
that horses buck, that rifles recoil, that widows cry,

that orphans stay orphans, that when it rains
the dusty streets turn to mud you might have to crawl
    through
with a bullet in your gut, that crawling through mud
with a bullet in your gut beats death or cowardice,

that gunshots crackle, that moustaches stay well oiled
even in a shootout, that when faced with superior odds
a good gunfighter cheats, and that Clint Eastwood
never dies. In the movies no one ever ages,

which is why that bandit in *The Good, The Bad, and The Ugly*
will forever stand atop a tombstone on tiptoes,
a noose around his neck, as the man with no name
gallops toward the orange Technicolor sunset

that tells me nothing about the true nature of dusk,
or the mercenary politics of American survival.

Brief Instructions for Writing an Outlaw Country Song about the Jena Six

Call the lily that grows in a gully
regret and croon toward her in the dark.
Call back the ghosts of your lynched ancestors.
Call back the ghosts that your ancestors lynched.
Call back the hurt you put on paradise
when the woman you loved left the earth
like a cut rose tossed on a compost heap.
Call back the twang of the termite, eating
empty coffins propped up before the showdown.
There is no gate in the gap between us
and God; even glory wears a long black veil.
There is no fence between heaven and hell.
There's a deep gulf that forms a chasm no man
can cross and no girl can lilt a song past.

Epithalamion Doused with Moonshine

The dead don't bivouac by the riverside.
I reckon love ain't two fifths consolation,
but a pint of bastard light through the gut.
I reckon our dead congregate, reeling
past the pointy steeple of paradise.
Be my *Oh Susanna, don't you cry for—*,
and I'll be your banjo's clawhammer strum.
We'll mainline sawdust and speak, in shotgun,
the language of *might coulds* juked in the dark.
I love you like gingham loves knobby knees.
Love me like a holster loves a warm gun.
Let angels lead us away while the catfish
are still in bloom and while we still reckon
some drunk mermaid's hit us with her flipper.

Irretrievable Cursives

I love the sloppy handwriting of rain
on windshields and my mother's
pirouetted loops on Hallmark cards.

I miss the arabesques my grandmother
described on lined loose leaf
and how my great grandmother transformed
the alphabet into a pack of jaunty fawns.

I love the off-kilter calligraphy
you practiced in your adolescent diaries
years before you met me, how you transcribed
Blake's eternal sunrise, his joys that fly,
as if sending a message to me across time.

I want to see the lost letters of Whitman
unfold their locomotive vowels
before my eyes and I imagine a perfect
poem has its own angelic cryptography,
but I haven't found it yet; it is hidden
somewhere inside the pigments of a Chagall,

or in the scrawl I will write when arthritis
gnarls my fingers and I try to remember
the magic of spelling my own name
for the first time in green ink on white paper,
when the world was a wagon pulled
by sparrows and I was already missing
all the phrases I would never be able to say.

Another Epic

I have lived in important places, times
      —Patrick Kavanagh

I could tell you everything that happened on Linden Street
the year the Berlin Wall fell. That was the year the Hanrahan
boy grew his hair to the middle of his back and rode his bike
down the block at 7 A.M. sharp every school day. The Perry
twins, with red hair longer than the Hanrahan boy's, vied
for the affections of Dino Taglione and the older girl won.
The pipes burst on 20 Linden and we lost the love letters my
grandmother had bundled in hatboxes and stored in a cor-
ner of the cellar. Masty Huba danced for loosies and beer
in front of the Brickyard Tavern all summer, and somebody
kept stealing the copper gutters off Saint Mary's rectory roof.
Monsignor Brigandi kept replacing them, and he would curse
and pray as he paced the block, throughout all the high holy
days of Ordinary Time, like Achilles in his tent.

A Benediction

When I close my eyes to pray, I picture my twelve year old
little brother on Linden Street in our grandfather's backyard,
the cowlick in his brown hair, the pants our mother patched
with paisley squares, his chubby cheeks, and his determined
look as he turned the dirt, flung eggshells on the soil, and
mended the chicken wire fence that surrounded the garden.
I want to write him a poem about our father's illness, our
mother's sadness, but I know he'd rather keep his emotions
locked in a cabinet where only he can hear them thump. I
keep thinking of the things we learned while we worked in
our grandfather's garden as he swore at us, called us block-
heads, smiled, and told us to *Mach Schnell* in a phrase he
picked up at the Battle of the Bulge. That backyard was our
grandfather's cathedral and there we learned all we needed to
know of holiness. There, his rusty toolshed was his altar, his
blood of Christ, cans of Ballantine beer. It was there that we
learned the sigh of shovels into earth can make a choir, labor
can break us into heavens, and curses can be prayers.

The Linden Street Card Club

A man is the sum of what women he knows.
            —Olivia Clare

My great grandmother, Nellie Mae Palermo, wore a silken
white slip as she ironed her nightgown in the living room.
My grandfather would say, "Shit Nellie, put some clothes on,"
but she would keep at it until the crinkles were gone, and
when she donned it she looked like a frail queen ready to play
cards with the ladies who gathered to gossip and play Tripoli
or Canasta, with their big hair, their Elizabeth Taylor per-
fume, and their Tupperware containers full of pennies, dimes,
and nickels. I loved those women with their dyed black or
blonde beehives, their uncontrollable laughter, their rosary
beads hanging from their purses, and their stories of a world
the size of the north side with streets that ran backward in
time. They, moored to1949, taught me to love women, who
could break at any moment into song, who endured diffi-
cult lives, harsh husbands, days of dusting dining rooms and
straightening mantles, whose voices lilted, lunged, and mes-
merized me, talking about what happened to the Hanrahan
boy down the street in 1975, talking about the nature of the
men they married, who went away to war and came back,
and worked and worked, and swore a lot, and drank more,
and raised families and died, talking about what desserts they
should bake for the Feast of the Assumption, talking about
the tabloid news Nellie Mae had just read in *The Enquir-
er*, about bigfoot sightings and Paul Newman's illegitimate
son, talking until I could feel their voices in my bones like
a lullaby rocking me forward, that I might understand the
importance of coming together, to laugh, to cry, to sing, to say
together a few simple words.

Thirteen

Middle school, like the novel, is a form
that encourages forgetting and so
I no more remember my daydreaming
of brown haired girls in algebra class
than I recall the dialogue between Vronsky
and Anna Karenina when she puts
him under her spell, but I know something
of the magical charm of atmospheres
and, therefore, I invoke the awkward
glory of being thirteen along with
drawing rooms and carriage rides where desire
builds a cage in the chest. God eludes me
too often, and somewhere in some country
someone is dying a horrible death
reserved for the just and the powerless.
Meanwhile, there are drone strikes. Obesity
occurs more frequently among the poor
in wealthy countries. Heroin use rises.
True, the high school kids I teach can barely
read cursive and some of them haven't read
a book in their whole lives, but so what?
They will no more remember a poem
than they will recall the cadence unsung
by ghost children toting Kalashnikovs.
Nevertheless, the miracle remains
that you were once a brown haired girl at work
on the arithmetic of passionate
scribbling, and despite the small cataclysms
that dot the path from thirteen to thirty,
I found you, awkward glory caged
in my chest, the damage of haste undone,
while the little bird in you kept chirping.

American Ark

In Kentucky, these guys are building an ark
exactly as God instructed Noah
and a few years ago there were these two
brothers in Burma who were ten years old,
leading this guerilla group, God's Army;
supposedly bullets couldn't harm them
and they commanded thousands of soldiers
invisible to the eye, but no less
deadly. Anyway, these are the stories
I might spin out, half remembered, for you
on a day like today when we're walking
over snow covered sidewalks in lazy
Saturday fashion. Today I mention
the ark again, how they can't quite figure
out what gopher wood is—I talk about
those twins in the jungle, how they could kill
by just pointing their rifles at the ground.
I wonder all the while if you're really alright,
after having gone to your mother's grave
just yesterday. In the Starbucks parking lot,
we look at a streetlight as you warm
the car and snow falls like invisible
soldiers or gnats that swarmed the animals
as they boarded that boat before the flood.
How lucky love makes us—that we might see
the simple miracle of snow falling
without irony and be grateful now
for a car whose heaters work, two coffees,
and no news of the world in all its strange
deluges, save the little wet halos
the flakes leave a moment after they melt.

Channeling Thelonious

Just because you're not the drummer,
doesn't mean you don't have to keep time,
doesn't mean time doesn't have to keep you
tisking, doesn't mean graveyard logic

proves America a theorem, doesn't mean
whiplashes and the feral tail of galaxies
become meaningless nightmares in the dark,
doesn't mean spinning around in circles

equals infinity or the KKK psychosis
of confiscated cabaret cards, doesn't mean
an elephant's at the keyboard, or the night
waltzes on less crepuscular without you,

doesn't mean shit, except that all you have
of heaven is a few chords the crickets
can't play right because they don't know
the changes, talking about post-racial this

and how Obama's supposed to make a sphere
where nobody hears that sick etude,
from just a few years ago, those chains made
on asphalt when James Byrd Jr.'s body

got dragged out in a national epistrophe.

A Hip Hop Generation History of My Heart

On the bus, we listened to Slick Rick, The Geto Boys,
and Big Daddy Kane. On the playground, we heard
the Beastie Boys and the Digital Underground.

At the dances in the middle school gym, we rocked
to Boyz II Men and Bel Biv Devoe. Iliana Arthur
and Yasharee White taught me the running man.

I had no rhythm, but I practiced, shuffling my feet
in the bathroom every night. At home, my mom
said any music that wasn't Aretha Franklin,

Roberta Flack, or James Taylor was probably
devil music. I started to mousse my hair back,
bought silk shirts and Cavaricci pants. I wanted

a gold rope chain with a big crucifix like the one
Malcolm Dixon wore when we played poker
and gin rummy for quarters in the janitor's closet.

I was in love with a girl who had a poof of hair
permanently aquanetted, like an arch, above
her forehead. She wore jelly shoes and carried

a Fendi bag. I doused myself in Drakkar Noir,
hid my baseball cards under my bed, and stopped
bringing my Fantastic Four comic books to class,

although I still read them at home, and secretly
wished I could cultivate Doctor Doom's iron
swagger. In eighth grade, when Jessica Green died

from a congenital heart defect, we all attempted
to be brave; we repeated the words our parents
had said about God having a plan and her being

in a better place, but I remember not believing
any of those things, and wondering why every kid
including myself, claimed Jessica as a best friend.

All the while, our parents' words came misshapen
from our mouths, music still boomed on the bus,
and in the playground we were becoming

what the heavy vowels and staccato beats of time
were awkwardly urging us to forever become.

Ode to Graffiti at the Lackawanna Train Depot

The mermaids no longer sing
northbound by rusted hulks
of the Norfolk Southern.

The drunken flipper of a god
wags across the tracks
as the night air whistles

past the old station. All
the hobos who once drifted
through town gobble

termites in their coffins
and neon clouds illuminate
the caboose of the moon.

The ghost of a feeling
is all we have left anymore
and that is why the magic

of the alphabet still holds
sway and the dominion
of midnight is subject

to the initials of bedraggled
taggers, who may never
see Chagall's flying brides,

but whose work carves
out a stained glass niche
in the behemoth cathedral

of an abandoned boxcar
upon which a globe
has been painted. No one

will circumnavigate it.
The fireflies that halo it
turn the train yard

into a mason jar the law
of wanton neglect shakes
into dazzles and shards.

An Idea of Heaven Proposed by the Ghost of Walt Whitman to the Ghost of Gerard Manley Hopkins as Overheard and Retold in the Spirit of Milton Kessler at the Closing of the Second to Last Independent Hardware Store in Broome County, New York

It is a place where the saints
always climb
the rickety old paint-splotched ladder
of the sky
as if they were day laborers
lumbering to the roof of a house
to rip old shingles off.
And inside that house
you're a sparrow
in the bird feeder section
of an endless Home Depot
you've flown into
without knowing why
and where, disoriented,
you peck at the crumbs
that might sustain you
through such unknowing,
only to be haloed
by an ordinary slant of sunlight
that flops itself
across the dirty floor you land on
before taking off
into the high rafters you will never reach,
your eternal reward
frozen in flight.

Channeling Sun Ra

Dear full moon, gripping nothing, testify
to the dry leaves, testify to the bridge
yawning over running waters that spin
no yarn about how to live a cosmos.

Pharaoh marshals his army in my chest.
When I chart the stars in my clavicle,
I draw the blueprints for the *Amistad*.
My heart pumps bilge water from the Red Sea.

I am, like any man, my own Moses.
I philosophize my tribe from twilight.
I break Birmingham into a model
of heliocentric unknowingness.

To presidents, I say democracy
travels interplanetary low ways.
Give me a mini moog to scrabble out
barrelhouse avatars of becoming.

If you look too long at the sorrow held
at the center of your life, you'll find no
choice, but to seek solace in the black keys
on a keyboard and the space between notes.

Dear rocket, grip oxygen, testify
to the fact that I am, like any man,
the off-kilter melody the wind makes
when it disturbs how Saturn spins in him.

The Lives of the Saints

Most were not recorded or canonized.
Of those, none received stigmata or healed
the sick. One could levitate after prayer,
but no one saw and she never confessed
this gift, even to her own parish priest.
One claimed that petting the soft brown muzzle
of her golden retriever offered God
more thanks than a thousand church litanies.
Another claimed watching a squirrel bungle
from tree to tree taught him all he could know
of holiness. The mystery of God's
will, said one, might be unlocked by taking
in, not the Eucharist, but a stray cat.
Most tended small gardens and held down jobs.
In the old days, some were farriers. Some worked
in shoe factories. Some were school teachers.
Some were housewives. Others, homeless. Some rode
the rails. Today, a few work at Walmart.
Some married. Some did not. All wed themselves
to life in the way that water beads on
treated flagstone or in the way the bee
courts the rhododendron blossom in May.
The weeping willow tree reminded one
of the Pietà. One saw angels in
his wife's hair. One saw his great grandmother's
face reflected in the baptismal font
at his daughter's baptism. Some were Catholic.
Most were not. Many died poor and alone.
All swam the world as sunlight through a school
of fish, glints in an ever shifting veil.

The New Pope Talks about
the Contents of His Briefcase

Asked what was in the black briefcase
that he carried onto the plane by himself
en route to Brazil, Francis said he had
a razor, a breviary, a book about St. Theresa,

a razor because favelas rise like stubble
all over the world, a razor because turning
the other cheek often exposes five o'clock
shadow, a razor because the meek

shall inherit the cutting instruments,
a razor because the meek shall inherit
the sting no styptic can staunch, a razor
because the sharp edge recalls Gethsemane

and Gethsemane is the world right now,
a breviary because prayer requires prompting
even among the holy, a simple breviary
because a flock forgets the shepherd's staff,

an ornate breviary because the basilica
of orchard, the basilica of forest and field,
obliges its priests to chant down the Babylon
of Rome, a breviary because the liturgy

always takes place in the dirtiest street,
a book about Saint Theresa of Avila
because recollection leads to devotion
and devotion leads to ecstasy, a book

about Saint Theresa because the prayer
of quiet culls a blessing from tears,
a book about Saint Theresa because if you
have God you will want for nothing,

a book about Theresa because the church
canonizes a new saint every minute
as if desperate to bludgeon us into heaven,
a razor, a breviary, a book about a saint,

because Christ has no body now on earth
but yours, and you have no baggage
now on earth save what nicks, what abridges,
what records, what beatifies what sorrow.

A Drone Pilot Discusses the Story of Abraham and Isaac

Faith is like a strip mall in the suburbs
of an unfamiliar town; you just drive
down the street and you can't miss it.

Once you've pulled in the parking lot,
you've got a sporting goods store,
a movie theater, and a TGIFriday's.

It's all one stop convenient like that.
You don't ever doubt that the Walmart
will carry the Tide marker you need

to get the coffee stain off your oxford.
You don't question the altar or the knife.
You don't mistake your son for a lamb.

You hear the dictates of the Lord
raging like a fire in a reed thicket
and you succumb to the logic of burning.

In fact, you praise flame; the burnt
offerings of your ancestors dance before
your eyes and you smell incense.

You know when you give the cashier
your debit card the transaction
will be approved; you never cross

your fingers hoping you won't be
embarrassed in the checkout line.
You never hope for a voice to come

rushing up the mountainside to halt you.
Even if the voice came, you wouldn't hear
because you are doing good work,

you are not breaking the covenant,
you are keeping your people safe,
and the blade levitates in your hand.

A Morning Prayer While Pumping Gas at the Gulf Station

Luke 24: 13–35

O my God, I offer you this small moment of attention
as I stare blankly at the KFC and the coin laundry
across the parkway, past the sign that says: "Life…
one mile at a time." I offer you the debit card swipe,
the numbers punched into the keypad, the nozzle lifted,
the gas cap twisted off, the lever flipped up, the clutch
of my hand on the pump, the rush of gallons through
the hose, and the flippant dance of dollars and cents
on the digital screen. I offer you what I don't heed:
this minute and a half when I am most myself
without care or desire as the cars rush by like a caravan
on the road to Damascus. I offer you the cement truck
that grunts up the hill, the teenager who blares Jay-Z
out the rolled down windows of his rusty Corolla.
I offer you the deserted parking lot across four lanes
of traffic and the new pizza place next door.
I offer you the bank sign that says "Horizons."
I offer you the smile of a little boy who waves to me
from the back seat of the Escalade about to pull away.
I offer you the quietness of moments like this,
the lull of the carwash, the lazy comfort of 6:40 A.M.
after I've pushed snooze on the alarm, before
it goes off again. I offer you the wind on my face
when I ride my bicycle downhill on a steep side street.
I offer you all the hours I don't check my cell phone.
I offer you all the minutes without Wi-Fi. I offer you
the wish for a world without Facebook, Twitter,
Guantanamo Bay, Enhanced Interrogation Techniques,
the war on terror, the drug war, the war on poverty.

I offer you the wish for a world without the one percent,
Occupy Wall Street, the Tea Party, the DNC, Fox News,
CNN, Netflix, waterboarding, Waco, Abu Ghraib.
I offer you the wish for a world without climate change,
global warming, Wiki-leaks, gentrification, Starbucks,
Walmart, Target, and the prison industrial complex.
O my dear Jesus, I offer you that old Zen phrase,
"If you meet the Buddha, kill the Buddha"
and without irony I offer you all of the moments
where life rolls out one mile at a time like the road
to Emmaus, where I am a stranger to myself,
where your incorruptible body lies broken and risen,
where I am unaware and graced by this unknowing,
where I am broken and can't help but rise closer to you.

Baby Jesus of the Washing Machine

Liam O'Leary told stories that scared
the entire fourth grade. He said the Blessed
Virgin Mary appeared in his closet.
Every night he went inside and closed the door.
He prayed the Hail Mary backwards, and then
she came, her blue dress bloodied, her rosy
body fading in and out of view. He also claimed
the baby Jesus lived in his washing
machine, spinning around with his mom's bras
and panties and his sister's dirty socks.
He said his mom used frankincense and myrrh
instead of fabric softener and detergent.
He insisted, "If you open the lid real quick,
you can see His halo swirling in the suds."

The Angel of Poetry

For, tho he cannot fly, he is an excellent clamberer.
        —Christopher Smart

Well done is better than well said.
        —Benjamin Franklin

Glory be the angel who opts not to use
his wings, who flings himself upon wet leaves
and stays, who wakes on earth and walks
around, who talks to those he meets
as if continuing a conversation after a short
awkward pause. Glory be he who doesn't
dwell on heaven, but is apt to ponder
the architecture of a single leaf. Glory be
the angel whose eyes stall on stars and start
on fireflies. Let him be grateful. Let him
listen. Let him stay small. For a penny saved
is like a fish between two cats. Glory be
the angel who wonders about life under
the ocean. Glory be he who wrote a poem
about a doorway he passed by and slipped
the paper it was written on down a sewer
grate as if he were mailing a letter. Glory be
the angel who understands how hard it is
to love your neighbor when your neighbor lives
next door. Glory be he whose wings twitch
while dreaming of flight, but who prefers
the work of earth to the comforts of sky,
and who knows that even angels age and die.

Chagall's Bride on the Leroy Street Bus

As I look out the window at the dirty streets
of my hometown, I wonder where the brides
are, the little crooked cottages thatched purple,
the levitating roosters and cows gashed with gold,
and the bulls and chickens that tornado to heaven
trailing vermillion while a bearded fiddler plays
and gypsy-looking women tip toward the sun.

The couples I see on Leroy Street are morbidly
obese and riding bicycles with plastic bags
full of groceries dangling from the handlebars.
They are not wed to the sky and dancing
the horizon in swaths of cerulean, dotted by
lamb's fleece, and choruses of cherubs, who pluck
at harps and laugh at the laws of gravity.

I would like for this place, Binghamton, NY,
to be exemplary and flying, but it's mostly
grubby looking and plain. However, the old lady
in the seat across the aisle looks like she's stepped,
midflight, off a canvas, with her plastic head cover
that protects a cadmium yellow dyed perm,
her beige orthopedic shoes stitched with viridian,

and her heavy winter coat, a shade just lighter
than ultramarine green. She could be an angel,
or my grandmother come back to life, framed
by a bus window dappled with cobalt blue rain.
Her head, jostled and bowing, rests against
the glass. She bounces as the bus bumps
over potholes and whips around corners.

Over her shoulder the drab streets go by,
a blur of now brilliant chimneys and roofs.
On her profile, the dim din of years slowly bursts
into flakes and flurries of chipped paint, her brow
a board, haloed and warped by choirs of snow.
When her stop comes, she pulls the cord
and glides down the aisle like a young girl,

who whirls as her veil trails over parquet floor.

Ode to Dumpster Sparrows near the Loading Dock at the Holiday Inn

They dive from the dock, skim asphalt, unpack
the secret of falling up to the rust
red russet sunburst tip, of the sky,
of the sigh, of garbage and God. They dip
down, genuflect, come correct, rustle scraps:
little abbots tending a cloistered garden
of grime, awash in shine of glistens
on gluten and congealed bacon fat,
broken mousetraps, used condoms, and crushed
cigarette packs. They transubstantiate
shards of shattered wine glasses agleam, globs
of daylight dinged by dust motes, and crud
encrusted soda bottle caps. Lost
in loose heaps, a-heave with heat of being
engaged, betrothed to the big wind, promised
this messy bliss, they revel in vomit
cleansed with Comet wrapped in Holiday Inn towels
and bloody bed sheets. Like miniature
mad scholars, they root among arcane scribbles
on pages torn from Gideon's Bible,
from the Book of Job, as if trying
to decipher ashes and fire and lines
about Lions devouring their pride.
Their wings lift like slips of discarded
registration paper blown in the breeze,
castigated to the cedars, summoned
to freeze in the lowest circle of hell
where the tiny bell of autumn never rings
and birds are forbidden to sing morning songs
of mourning for dawn's passing. They swoop,
searching for the true host, the body

and blood in rye crusts, those chunks half-sopped
in lentil soup. They venerate the stale bread
in beaks, unfettered flight fused to desire.
Finally, when they eat the crusts, the arks
of their bodies turn to flying, and scatter,
fleeting as vows from lips of those too young
to know the weight of what they say.

What I Didn't Learn about Reading in High School

That meaning rests in the margins and waits
to waylay you, that music is a verb
and verbs waltz like the Russian debutantes
in a Tolstoy novel, that all reading
is misreading and re-reading what's been
misread, that misreading is the highest
form of writing, that words are more akin
in their couplings to a Chagall painting
than to a Jackson Pollack—see them fly
above the thatched cottages with the angels,
the lovers, and the livestock—that your ears
read more than your eyes ever could, that smell,
touch, and taste might help you to navigate
the page, that your heartbeat when you're reading
a line of Whitman does more work than eyes
and mind together, that all gerunds are
bicyclists in the *Tour de France*, that nouns
are dollhouse cathedrals without bishops,
that a word spoken lives eternities
in air before it alights on paper
again, that all print is a form of braille
and all readers are more blind than Milton
or Borges, that conjunctions are the stems
the sap shoots through, that a gap in the text
presages resurrection or works like
a flock of doves in the belly, that I
am not the I who reads this line, but have
become a cardinal in these branches,
that conversation is the most ignored
form of reading—listen to the moonlight
discourse on the pasture fence and talk to

the stray cat meowing around your front porch—
that stories have warbled us all into
being, that being requires retelling
the sorrows of the locust tree, the joys
of the ladybug, and the constancy
of the sparrow showering in the dirt,
that a book is a lullaby the wind
ricochets off tombstones, that a poem
is a canoe—paddle with me—we will
brush the leaf off, the web off, decay off,
this ink, our commerce, this meaning, the page.

Speculations Implicit in the
Motion of an Ant's Mandibles

The universe is made of stories,/ not of atoms.
   —Muriel Rukeyser

A story's a cosmos packed in atoms.
A body's clauses are predicative.
The codswallop the dew spits built morning.
Dusk's when we wait for the stars' malarkey.
Rhetoric's what makes a calyx ragged.
Cursing shakes loose the roots of daffodils.
The maul splits the cordwood into crooning.
Hokum's what the wind tells the hickory.
The bullfrog robs the fen of its pathos.
One warble could unhouse a life of flight.
I walk a line crayoned by wren's song.
The sky speaks the jargon of aerospace.
Formulae hop from burrow to burrow.
The grasshopper doubles as helix.
The clouds do not contain electrolytes.
I will die, as will the blue barn swallow.
A blue-tipped wing equals a dynasty.
The apple's a monarch of branch and air.
An orchard's an empire in late autumn.
I will tell my grief to the plain poplar.
A single gaze does the work of termites.
No gust matters save what rustles woodbine.
The crow sides with the incantatory.
Even the turtledove steals an ethos.
I will build a nest inside the blackbird.
The bird's belly contains the cud's cooing.
Prophecy comes from the ox's fourth gut.
Sparrows prove the theorem of windowpanes.

To dance is to be more than mere cut worm.
Intuition forgives the harrow's comb.
Death makes a honeycomb. Pull out the bee.
Art is what rebukes the subtle hive so.
Poetry's an art as mild as watching
a paper cup bobbing in the river.
Archimedes discovered buoyancy
while getting into a tub, but the screw
came from seeing dust motes thread a doorframe.
The universe is made not of stories,
but of fragmentary soliloquies
that lend the moth insane for light its logos.

Bridge Work at the Confluence of the Susquehanna and Chenango Rivers

I see the joy of 2:25 p.m. with no place to be, breeze through
the leaves of the blueprints the construction crew foreman has
placed under a cinderblock on a bulldozer's tread. I watch the
current like a vagrant fisherman, like the old guy I see strut-
ting with his shirt off, an eagle tattoo taking flight from his bi-
cep, with his five gallon plastic paint bucket, rusty tackle box,
and Salvation Army rod, who casts for hours in the hot sun,
trying to snag a trout from the dirty mouth of the Susquehan-
na, but who only catches a buzz off the malt liquor he drinks
from a bottle in a brown paper bag. I'd like to be as ragged as
this guy, to let my hair gray and grow long, to swagger around
with my gut swinging, and to court the Chenango all after-
noon. Between me and this guy, there's a world of unfinished
bridges, pints of bourbon through the liver, and hellbenders
squirming through mud, but we are both here wedding our-
selves to the water of two rivers as workers rehab the bridge's
crumbling pylons. We watch a Styrofoam cup come to the
small dam, dip under the foam, and float on. It goes the way
these wrists of clay dictate. It is there, buoyant as the impulse
that skims a prayer from nowhere and makes of breath a bare
linden tree in winter. Blessed be what idles, but moves forever
restless, the debris that churns for a time in wild waters.

Driving Around

after Pablo Neruda

Today, driving on Main Street I passed a man in a cowboy hat
with a ragged blanket draped around him like the cape of a
roman soldier, slouching in the heat of the sun. I saw another
man, who wore a pink bicycle helmet and pushed a shopping
cart full of bottles and cans. Two fat old women in motorized
wheelchairs, racing up the middle of the road, held traffic
to a crawl. A girl, with a leashed ferret perched atop her left
shoulder, stood on the corner of Glenwood Boulevard and
Main. The owner of the Matin Food Mart on Front Street
shooed a bum from his stoop as I waited for the light to turn.
My thoughts turned to the Rilke poem about the panther
pacing in its cage at the Paris zoo, that beast who could see no
world beyond its bars. I thought I'd write a poem that com-
pares Rilke's animal to the people I see in Binghamton, New
York, with their Sabbath faces, their tense, arrested muscles,
and their ritual dances down Court Street, fueled by alcohol
and poverty, but then I was ashamed of myself and of Rilke's
influence. I was ashamed for thinking I could force their
stories forward instead of letting them be as they are: leashing
their faith in the real to their wrists, racing up the street after
the unknown, slouching toward the afternoon sun, or Chapin
Street, or a holy mystery of which I'm unaware, more tangible
than a poem, or a panther, or a poem about a panther, holi-
est in the impulse, to live, to praise, and to die in doubt. It so
happens that I'm not tired of being a man, and although some
days I'd like to tattoo teardrops on my cheek, I have no need
to cut lilies or to run through the streets with a green knife. I
drive past closed law offices and forgotten shoe shops, aban-
doned factories, and halal delis selling goat meat. The bras on
clotheslines on Leroy Street never weep.

Sometimes I Think I'll Never Leave the Triple Cities

after César Vallejo

I imagine I'll die at 65, on a Tuesday, at 2 in the afternoon, teaching a bunch of rowdy 9th grade angels Shakespeare's sonnet 130, having traveled no farther than Johnson City, NY, for years.

I imagine I'll die on a Tuesday in Endicott, NY, on a rainy day in October, just after the leaves have turned. I imagine I'll die wondering where all the shops have gone from my childhood.

The Triple Cities School of Beauty Culture, where my grand-mother used to get her hair done, after shopping for dangly earrings at Boscov's Department Store, has been turned into a bookshop and when I die on a Tuesday, in Endicott, NY, 32 years from now, no one will remember the beauticians in training with their purple smocks, who smoked cigarettes in front of the parole office on their breaks.

When I die at 2 in the afternoon, no one will remember the beauty school sign and how it used to seem the center of hills breaking into autumn. No one will remember how my grand-mother smiled with her platinum blonde perm and thinning hair, how after years of a jet black beehive, she used to say that she'd decided to look like Marilyn Monroe for my grandfather.

When I die on a Tuesday, in the dirty city of Endicott, NY, no one will remember the old Sicilians who came there to work in the EJ shoe factory. The 9th graders I teach will never know how beatific my grandmother looked with her gaudy earrings, a fresh perm, and a shopping bag under her arm, as she coasted along the broken sidewalks of Court Street.

I imagine I'll die on a rainy Tuesday, in my October class-room, at age 65, at 2 in the afternoon, in Endicott, NY, in love with the poetry in the petals of those future students' faces, and with my last breath I will tell them, and with my last breath I will tell them, and with my last breath I will tell them: this place, these ghosts, those people, that I love are nothing like the sun.

After Reading Emerson's
"Woods, A Prose Sonnet"

I have no wisdom and no woods to walk in, no acorn on the
oak and no time to talisman my pocket. There is no whistle
to wren me into pyrola bud, no breeze to maple me into the
eternal. Autumn doesn't redden anymore here and nobody
praises the sacred. No one asks the pines or rains or brooks or
birds for their music anymore. Instead, a plastic ball on a lawn
rolls toward a road with dandelions for mile markers. Now,
the wind's forever unhoused by silly conjectures of dipping
sycamores and I admit that pain is real. However, I've forgot-
ten the lessons of first snow and a bee sting on my bare foot
no longer throbs like a blessing. Still, I want to wed myself to
an absent wilderness, to a backwoods where form is not com-
pletely flattened out, to a boondocks where melody continues
to matter, not because it's pretty or because it carries meaning,
but because it is. Give me nature not as organizing principle,
not as source of song, but as tangle of badland scrub brush
and rough country ragweed where gale breaks brambles into
a sway that does not have to dance in order to be beautiful.
Better yet, give me sewer grates and sidewalks to mediate my
ignorance of the divine.

Like Those Pictures of Breughel that Make of the Profound a Pinprick and Those Poems of Williams that Break Cut Roses into Stars

I'm tired of amazing things: the wren blended into eternity, its warble elevated into psalm.

I'd rather have back the voices of my parents arguing in another room as I lay with the covers over my head, listening to a Mets game on the radio.

Outside my bedroom, it was 1986 and there was no accounting for the universe, no knowledge of art, save the stippling in the arc made by Captain America's shield as it ricocheted off the Red Skull's chest.

I was unaware of the Milky Way above my house at night and in the afternoons I played in the dirt, trying to understand the thesis implied by a trail of ants.

Of course, in a story time takes no time and years passed. I pulled a bee from the rose. Azaleas bloomed and wilted. Factories closed. The city cut down most of the linden trees on Linden Street.

I love the sound of passing freight trains and running water. Life is not that hard, my friend. Watch a squirrel bound through a field of snow. Love.

Someday, I want to make my hands a cup and drink water from a mountain brook.

Self-Portrait as Don Cherry Praying to Saint Cecilia

Music is a verb.
　　　—Ornette Coleman

'Cause the moon and I have flirted before,
the stars stand arms akimbo and because
the earth calls me kindred, the heavens won't

accept my calls. I admit I've called at
odd hours and perhaps too late. However,
I'm running down the scales. I'm running through

a Miles Davis number, running down hours,
threading noontime with filaments of brass.
I skitter on the edge of the unknown.

I cleave a sweet sound in two and corset
the melody a stone makes when it's flung;
Angel, teach me the song of subway cars.

Angel, instruct me in the harmony
that whistles along turnpikes and off-ramps.
Angel, let music conquer my stillness.

My glissando martyrs me with moonlight.
I growl. I flutter tongue. I triple tongue
a feeling back into the unsayable.

I gusset. I dry gulch. I heave and spin.
My vibrato builds a minaret from
empty minutes and I climb to its crown.

I fling crescendos from doorways, thresholds,
sweep the sills with trills of my one true tone,
homesickness; I vacate the quiet with my cry.

One long cinder strand winds its way through day,
says goodbye, hangs there, suspended in air,
babbles on a note, a leaf in wind that will not fall.

Captain America Talks to Emma Lazarus after Reading Toni Morrison's *Tar Baby*

I used to think we were made of water,
atoms, and the stories old ladies tell
each other while they're waiting for tea
to steep. The tea was orange pekoe
and those old ladies, our grandmothers,
chattered away the early afternoon,
gossiping huddled masses to grim bulwarks,
talking 1776 minus 1492 equals the curse
of Ham minus the first of January, 1863,
divided by Denmark Vesey and the ghost
of Crispus Attucks, which is the same
equation used to solve for Malcolm X
or the Stonewall Riots multiplied by Waco,
Ruby Ridge, Abner Louima, the fifteenth
of September, 1963, and Amadou Diallo.
I used to think the Battle of the Bulge
made up for the Battle of Little Big Horn,
but that's like calling the moon a hubcap
and trying to pry it off with a copper torch.
When I look at that famous old painting
of George Washington crossing the Delaware,
I see King Boabdil leaving Granada in tears.
Valley Forge is my Guernica. 9/11
is my 9/11. I used to think Wounded Knee
ended Bo Jackson's career, but it turned out
that was a hip injury. I get my news
from Pharaoh's army and the plague of frogs.
When I look at the stars on the flag I see
Sojourner Truth saying: "Ain't I a woman."
I mistake Frederick Douglass for Einstein
and vice versa. Pictures of Teddy Roosevelt

shooting a buffalo adorn my dishtowels.
The Department of Homeland Security
confiscated my grandmother's sugar bowl.
The fourth of July is my Groundhog's Day.
I no longer believe in uniforms, iambic feet
that feel the fell of dark not day, or using
patriotism as a shield. Give me rags, give me
spondees (football, D-Day, black holes),
give me a perfectly timed somersault
over a Humvee in Kandahar Province.
Dear Emma, mother of exiles, I lift my lamp
beside the golden door and tell you
I am that great mass of undocumented men,
the Huck Finns, the drifting Jims, angels
lost in the backwater arithmetic of empire.

After Listening to Obama's Immigration Speech I Pray to Saint Jesús Malverde

People not trapped by our past, but able to remake ourselves as we choose.
          —Barrack Obama (2014)

Vivas to those who have failed.
          —Walt Whitman (1855) as quoted by Martín Espada
          (2014)

I wonder if it's possible to not
let the past splinter our infinitives,
to bravely remake ourselves in this vast
mesa, this America, where coyote
chases field mouse and others pack bodies
in vans bound for Laredo or Houston,
and how to prioritize the bullwhip
logic of exclusion as a pathway
to citizenship, but our concern lies
equally with felon and family,
with criminal and child, with gang member
and single mom. I'll never understand
how it can be made illegal to be,
how the promise of freedom can become
twenty to a trailer and a rooster
in the yard. I crow, in kilos, a prayer
for a new understanding of struggle.
We stay strangers even after we've crossed
Atlantic, Pacific, and Rio Grande;
We stay strangers toting guns in Kabul,
flying up Fifth Avenue in our cabs,
working a quarry in Susquehanna,
washing dishes in a Flagstaff diner,
paying off our daughters' school loans.

Today, I'm praying for an amnesty
that doesn't turn a child into a gap
in a government document, a scrawl
graffitied on a passing freight train car.
Our bullets are asleep in their chambers;
Tonight, I look at the water of our rivers
inscribed with an *e pluribus unum,*
and to those waters, from those holy words,
I whisper *salve, bienvenidos,*
huānyíng guānglín, ahlan wa sahlan,
welcome, and *vivas* for those who have failed
to mortise a foothold in our granite,
but who tendon themselves with their striving.

A Breviary for the Liturgy of Leroy Street

Learn how to pray in the dirtiest street,
the boulevard with the closed carpet store
where mattresses lean on telephone poles
and wooden spools serve as picnic tables.
Learn how to pray outside at two o'clock
in the afternoon when the sidewalks teem
with no pedestrian except the ants
that stream from lawnless apartment house yards.

Make your tongue a temple bell that rings
for the lonely and the unsatisfied,
for those bound to the opposite of song,
for those who wander the aisles of Walmart,
for those who prefer Target and Sam's Club,
for those whose bath soap has hair stuck in it,
for those who sip vanilla soy lattes
at Starbucks, for those who go to the black
light eighties nights at Applebees, who drink
apple martinis, who watch NFL
games every weekend, and who dream touchdowns.
Learn how to pray in the dirtiest street
because the church is boarded up and you
are a broken wafer without barcode;
You are a chorus singing "Amazing Grace"
to a crowd of teenagers whose earbuds
drown out *how sweet the sound that saved a wretch*
like me in the dirtiest street, which feels
like a monastery where all the monks
have taken a vow of deafness, a vow
to be like a fire that consumes itself
because it never turns outward. To pray

means learning to listen to one whisper
the wind makes when it whips through linden leaves
on a street that's forgotten your last name.

Learn how to pray in the dirtiest street
because no immaculate pew will wrest back
holiness from the saints and bring it down
where it belongs, right here on Leroy Street,
among these ordinary ill angels
who drink warm beer on their porches and bitch
about how their wives stole their halos and sold
them, with their wings, for a few dollars,
plus postage, to the Vatican online.

Elegy for Philip Levine

If you're old enough to read this you know
what work isn't; it isn't in poems
or in the screed a screen door delivers
when it opens and bangs shut on your thoughts
of childhood. You might even agree that
the opening salvo of "West End Blues"
matters more than anything you could write
in seven lifetimes, but so what, my friend.
Out of burlap sacks, out of kiss my ass,
we say goodbye as the factories close,
and our amber waves of grain have become
yellow lines in a Walmart parking lot.
However your life unfolded, it was
an enormous yes, gathering milkweed,
sweet will, winter words, dust, and red carnations
to scatter on the graves of dictators
as an imprecation and a warning.
Now America shackles amendments
to tailpipes and all the bluebirds' windpipes
are cut to whistling so long or "Dixie."
Our love, your rose's many thorns, the dew
that won't wait long enough to stand your wren
a drink, the no one who listened to wind
speak its new truth to the moon—all are gone,
jacketed in a guttural moan off
the coast of a distant Ellis Island.
What actually took place is now lost
in the mythologies of families,
yoking stories to the dinner table,
aproning them there into immense sails,
beat in time to the pulse felt at the wrist.

We'll never waken on a world again
where your Detroit of '48 will be
carried and transmuted—those oily floors,
those fathers departed in fifth autumns,
those torn into light and underbellied
in stone, those cartwheels into early dusk
now become a poem with no ending.

Words for Barbara, Many Years From Now

Remember that once you rode not a horse,
on the carousel, but a neigh that bucked
and whinnied into the teeth of the big
wind whipping around your ears; during those
days you drank water with a fork and danced
to a brass band playing "Just a Closer
Walk with Thee." Remember that for a time
you were two and mightier than sunlight's
shimmer on ripples bum rushing the past.
Remember the sneeze of a small monkey
in the zoo once made you laugh and this was
all one could hope to learn of poetry.
Remember that once, before you grew up,
you rode the neighs written deep in our bones.

About the Writer

Dante Di Stefano's poetry, essays, and reviews have appeared in *Brilliant Corners, Iron Horse Literary Review, The Los Angeles Review, New Orleans Review, Obsidian, Prairie Schooner, Shenandoah, The Writer's Chronicle*, and elsewhere. He was the winner of the Thayer Fellowship in the Arts, The Red Hen Press Poetry Award, The *Crab Orchard Review's* Special Issue Feature Award in Poetry, The Allen Ginsberg Poetry Award, The Ruth Stone Poetry Prize, The Phyllis Smart-Young Prize in Poetry, The Bea González Prize in Poetry, and an Academy of American Poets College Prize. He is a correspondent for *The Best American Poetry Blog* and the poetry book review editor for *Arcadia*. He earned his PhD in Poetry from Binghamton University and he lives in Endwell, New York.

Acknowledgments

Many thanks to the editors of the following print and online journals in which poems from this collection were first published:

2 Bridges Review: "Statue of the Emaciated Buddha"

Amethyst Arsenic: "A Drone Pilot Discusses the Story of Abraham and Isaac"

Arcadia: "The Lives of the Saints"

Atticus Review: "Filibuster to Delay the Death of My Father"

Bayou Magazine: "Chemotherapy Epithalamion"

Big Muddy: "A Carpetbagger's Guide to Holly Springs, Mississippi"

Black Heart Magazine: "Like Those Pictures of Breughel that Make of the Profound a Pinprick and Those Poems of Williams that Break Cut Roses into Stars" and "Words for Barbara, Many Years from Now"

Blinders Literary Journal: "Let the Mermaids Flirt with Me"

The Blue Earth Review: "Driving Around"

Booth: "Without Wings"

Brevity: "Another Epic"

Brilliant Corners: "Channeling Mingus"

The Chiron Review: "Making a Canoe Out of the Eden Tree"

The Comstock Review: "Baby Jesus of the Washing Machine"

Connecticut River Review: "From Nightlight Past Midnight Moon to Hospital Hallway and Back Again" and "Ode to Graffiti at the Lackawanna Train Depot"

Dappled Things: "The New Pope Talks about the Contents of His Briefcase"

Dialogist: "If I Did Not Understand the Glory and Suffering of the Human Heart I Would Not Speak Before Its Holiness"

Duende: "Brief Instructions for Writing an Outlaw Country Song about the Jena Six"

Gris-Gris: "A Breviary for the Liturgy of Leroy Street," "Channeling Nina Simone," "Channeling Thelonious," and "Your Freckles Compared to a Muddy Waters Song"

The Grove Review: "Seventeen"

Hawai'i Pacific Review: "American Ark"

The Hollins Critic: "The Orchard Keeper"

Hunger Mountain: "Epithalamion Doused with Moonshine"

Italian Americana: "Dancing in the Parking Lot of the *Prefabricati*"

The James Franco Review: "Stephen Hawking Warns Artificial Intelligence Could End Mankind"

Journal of Language and Literacy Education: "What I Didn't Learn about Reading in High School"

The Journal of Sustainability Education: "After Reading Emerson's 'Woods, A Prose Sonnet'"

Kudzu House Quarterly: "An Idea of Heaven Proposed by the Ghost of Walt Whitman to the Ghost of Gerard Manley Hopkins as Over-heard and Retold in the Spirit of Milton Kessler at the Closing of the Second to Last Independent Hardware Store in Broome County, New York"

The Madison Review: "Speculations Implicit in the Motion of an Ant's Mandibles"

Mastodon Dentist: "With a Coat"

Naugatuck River Review: "A Defense of Confessional Poetry" appeared as "Last Rites"

Obsidian: "Channeling Sun Ra," "Self-Portrait as Don Cherry Praying to Saint Cecilia," and "While Listening to Professor Longhair I Imagine the Atoms in the Flowers of a Winter Cherry Outside my Window-sill and I Know Everything's Gonna Be Alright"

Paddlefish: "Chagall's Bride on the Leroy Street Bus"

Paterson Literary Review: "Fighting Weather," "A Morning Prayer While Pumping Gas at the Gulf Station," and "Sometimes I Think I'll Never Leave the Triple Cities"

Pembroke Magazine: "A Hip Hop Generation History of My Heart"

Quarter After Eight: "Accident Report"

Ragazine: "The Angel of Poetry," "Benny," and "Field Trip"

Rattle Online: "Elegy for Philip Levine"

The Sierra Nevada Review: "After Listening to Obama's Immigration Speech I Pray to Saint Jesús Malverde" and "Channeling Coltrane"

South Dakota Review: "What I Learned from Spaghetti Westerns"

Southern California Review: "Ode to Dumpster Sparrows near the Loading Dock at the Holiday Inn"

The Southampton Review: "Thirteen"

Stoneboat: "If I Were a Character in a Rural Noir I'd Learn Claw Hammer Banjo and Mourn the Slow Betrayal of the Body that Inevitably Occurs in Life Outside of Novels"

Stone Canoe: "Bridge Work at the Confluence of the Susquehanna and Chenango Rivers" and "Irretrievable Cursives"

VIA: Voices in Italian Americana: "A Benediction"

"Bridge Work at the Confluence of the Susquehanna and Chenango Rivers" and "Irretrievable Cursives" were selected by Bruce Bennet as the winners of the 2015 Bea González Prize for Poetry

"Epithalamion Doused with Moonshine" was selected by Michael Dickman as the winner of the 2014 Ruth Stone Poetry Prize

"A Morning Prayer While Pumping Gas at the Gulf Station" won second place in the 2014 Allen Ginsberg Poetry Awards

"Speculations Implicit in the Motion of an Ant's Mandibles" won the 2014 Phyllis Smart-Young Prize in Poetry

"Sometimes I Think I'll Never Leave the Triple Cities" won first place in the 2012 Allen Ginsberg Poetry Awards

Many thanks, as well, to the editors of the following anthologies in which poems from this collection were included:

The Great Falls: An Anthology of Poems about Paterson, New Jersey (The Poetry Center Press, 2014): "Love is a Stone Endlessly in Flight"

It Was Written: Poetry Inspired by Hip Hop (Minor Arcana Press, 2016): "Captain America Talks to Emma Lazarus after Reading Toni Morrison's *Tar Baby*"

The Orison Anthology (Orison Books, 2016): "If I Did Not Understand the Glory and Suffering of the Human Heart I Would Not Speak Before Its Holiness"

The Poetry Storehouse (The Poetry Storehouse Online, 2014): "Channeling Mingus," "Channeling Thelonious," "Dancing in the Parking Lot of the *Prefabricati*," "The Orchard Keeper," and "Statue of the Emaciated Buddha"

Till the Tide: An Anthology of Mermaid Poetry (Sundress Publications, 2015): "Epithalamion Doused with Moonshine"

I would also like to thank my family and friends, coauthors all of the poems in this book. I am particularly grateful to my mother, Donna Di Stefano, to my brother, Daeman Di Stefano; to the Rizzo family, especially Fred and Barbara; to my sisters-in-law, Billie, Lisa, and Melanie; to my publishers, Jonis Agee and Brent Spencer; to my friends, Stephen "Birddog" Blabac, the Boumans (Nat, Katherine, Harper, Nina, and Gus & Tom, Emily, and Barbara), Tera Buckley, Elizabeth Denman, Deanna Dorangrichia, and Nicole Santalucia; to my teachers at Binghamton University, Martin Bidney, Paul-William and Beth Burch, Joseph Church, Salvador Fajardo, Joseph Keith, Maria Mazziotti Gillan, Liz Rosenberg, Karin Terebessey, Libby Tucker, and Joe Weil; to my students; and, most of all, to my lovely wife, Christina, my first and best reader and the starting point for many of the poems contained herein.

CPSIA information can be obtained
at www.ICGtesting.com
Printed in the USA
BVOW08s0419251016

465936BV00001B/10/P